Salamander Surprise!

Written by Jennifer Beck
Illustrated by Ian Forss

Flying Start
to Literacy®

Contents

Chapter 1
Pet Day

I could hardly wait to get to school that morning. Ever since our class had been given the notice about Pet Day, I'd been looking forward to showing Goldie to my friends.

Dad hadn't really wanted to buy me a dog, especially a labrador. He said they eat a lot, and sometimes they wander off in search of food. But I kept asking, and in the end Dad said I could have a dog.

Luckily we've got a big yard with plenty of room for a dog to run around. I just have to be careful to keep the gate shut so Goldie doesn't get out onto the road.

"You're gorgeous," I whispered as I brushed Goldie's gleaming coat. I wanted Goldie to look his best for Pet Day.

"Everyone at school will be so jealous of my pet!" I whispered to him.

On the way to school, I met Isabella, coming out of her house. Isabella's in my class.

You should have seen Isabella's face when she saw Goldie. She was really excited.

"I didn't know you had a dog! What's his name?" she said.

"Goldie. He's a pure-bred labrador. Want to pat him?"

"I'd love to!" said Isabella, bending down and carefully placing the plastic box she'd been carrying on the footpath.

"He's beautiful," she whispered, gently stroking Goldie's head.

I told her that when Goldie's older I'll be taking him to dog shows, and he's sure to win a lot of prizes.

I thought I'd better ask about Isabella's pet.

"What have you got in that box?" I said.

Isabella smiled. "I call him Sam."

She lifted the lid. Lying in some weeds was the weirdest-looking creature I've ever seen! It was yellow and black with big eyes and a long tail.

"Yuck!" I screamed, jumping back and nearly tripping over Goldie's leash. "What is it? A lizard?"

Isabella laughed. "No, Sam's a salamander. I'll take him out when we get to school, then you can have a better look at him!"

I didn't know what to say – I really didn't want to touch an ugly creature like that.

I was glad when we got to school and I could leave Isabella and show Goldie to my friends.

Chapter 2
What a disaster!

As it turned out, Pet Day was a disaster. Goldie got excited during the Grand Parade and had a fight with Andy Shaw's dog. His scruffy little dog started it of course, then Andy told me I needed to take Goldie to obedience classes!

Afterwards, back in class, things got worse. Everyone took turns talking about their pets. While I was telling the class that Goldie's father won Grand Champion at the National Dog Show, I noticed some kids laughing and pointing at Goldie.

I turned around and saw that he had my pencil case in his mouth and was shaking it around, making pencils fly everywhere. When I tried to take it from him, he started running around the classroom!

Everyone was laughing!

When Miss Fisher finally settled the class down, I had to listen to everyone else talk about boring pets like birds and guinea pigs.

Then Isabella stood up to talk about her salamander.

Great, I thought. Now everyone will be really bored!

But they weren't bored. They seemed to find her talk interesting!

Isabella said that salamanders had been on Earth since the time of the dinosaurs. She's got a few of the weird creatures, and keeps them at home in a glass tank called a vivarium. (I only remember that because Miss Fisher wrote the word on a chart.)

"Some salamanders are smaller than my little finger," Isabella said, holding up her hand. "Others, like the Japanese giant salamander, can weigh as much as a person – but I haven't got one of those."

That made the class laugh. But it was a good sort of laughing – not the way they had laughed at me and Goldie.

Isabella went on and on, holding up a picture of some salamander from Mexico that's a protected species. How boring!

"Who'd want one of those for a pet?" I whispered.

But the other kids seemed fascinated.

"Why is it that whitish colour?"

"What are those pink frilly things around its neck?"

Finally Isabella finished talking. But then Miss Fisher said, "For science next week we're going to study amphibians. Isabella, could you bring some of your salamanders to school? Then the class could observe them, and you could tell us even more about them."

Oh, no! Why did we have to hear more about ugly lizards – my Goldie was much more beautiful and interesting.

I was glad when Pet Day was over and I could play fetch with Goldie in our yard. Afterwards, he curled up next to me while I watched my favourite TV show.

You couldn't do that with a salamander!

Chapter 3
Missing salamander

The next week, Isabella's vivarium became the centre of attention. And Isabella got to give us another talk. She told the class about all the different tricks salamanders have learned to help them survive.

"Some can survive fires by running through the flames," she said. "They produce a kind of foam or mucus that protects their skin from the heat."

"Wow!" said the kids in the front row.

"Yeah, and when it dries, they scrape it off with their feet," said Isabella.

"Eww!" I said loudly. "That's disgusting!"

"And some salamanders drop their tails when they are in danger," Isabella went on. "When they do this, their tails keep wriggling, which distracts a predator and allows the salamander to escape."

"Cool!" shouted Andy Shaw and his friends.

"Ugh!" I muttered.

The next day we got a big shock when we arrived at school. Our classroom had been broken into overnight. Some of our class computers were stolen. Nothing else was missing, but some water had been tipped out of the vivarium and stones and plants had been thrown around the room. It was a mess.

Isabella rushed over to check on her salamanders. She found one was missing.

"It's Sam!" she cried. "He's gone! Maybe he's hiding somewhere. He could starve! Please help me find him!"

Miss Fisher said that we all had to help look for Sam. It was disgusting. We had to crawl around under the desks, and check behind the shelves and inside the cupboards.

The class searched everywhere, but nobody could find Sam. Isabella looked very upset at the end of the day when it was time to go home without him.

The truth was, I was feeling a bit guilty.

I'd looked in the corridor outside our classroom, behind the drinking fountain. It was next to some cupboards so I had to crouch down to see behind it.   Right at the back where a pipe was leaking, I'd glimpsed a quick movement like a flick of a tail.

I was pretty sure it was Sam, but I hadn't said anything.

I was still annoyed that Isabella and her silly salamander got all the attention on Pet Day instead of Goldie and me.

Isabella can suffer a bit longer, I thought. Tomorrow I would pretend to discover Sam, and everyone would be proud of me.

Chapter 4
Pet rescue

In the morning I was still feeling guilty, so I decided to walk to school with Isabella. I waited outside her house.

When I saw her, she looked worried. I thought she was still sad about Sam, but then she suddenly pointed behind me.

I turned around and my heart almost stopped. There was Goldie, running loose down the footpath across the street!

I'd been in a grumpy mood when I left home that morning – had I forgotten to shut the gate? Our neighbour had just put out his wheelie bin. Maybe Goldie smelled something and ran out of the yard.

I looked down the street. At the end there
was a main road, with trucks zooming past.
Goldie was headed right for that road.

"Goldie! Come back!" I shouted, but Isabella
was faster. Before I could move she'd
crossed the street, raced after Goldie, and
grabbed him by the collar.

Goldie could have been killed!

When I tried to thank Isabella, she just shrugged it off and gave Goldie a hug.

"I didn't want you to lose your lovely pet," she said.

You can just imagine how I felt then. I'd been mean to Isabella and now she'd saved my pet's life!

I burst into tears.

"I'm so sorry about Sam!" I blurted out. "I was jealous of all the attention you and your salamanders were getting. I think I know where Sam could be. I'll just put Goldie back in our yard, then let's get to school."

Sure enough, the little salamander was hiding in the damp space behind the drinking fountain. Isabella didn't ask any questions. She was just so happy to find Sam alive and unharmed. That day after school I helped her carry the vivarium back home, and we've been good friends ever since.

On sunny days Isabella and I take Goldie
for a walk together, and on wet days
I sometimes go to Isabella's place and help
her look after her salamanders. Sometimes
we catch worms and insects for them to eat.

Now I think that salamanders are amazing
creatures, but I haven't actually picked one
up yet – I'm scared it might drop its
wriggling tail!

A note from the author

The idea of a salamander as a pet goes back to my first year as a teacher. A child in my class brought a Mexican axolotl to school. I'd never seen a salamander before, and that's when I first learned a little about them. Through researching this story I now know a lot more about these amazing and adaptable creatures.

School Pet Days are fun, but the combination of excited children and a variety of pets can also lead to trouble. Some children can become jealous if someone else's pet gets all the attention. However, pets can also help create friendships as children can share the joy of looking after a pet.